# Tim has a net and a can.

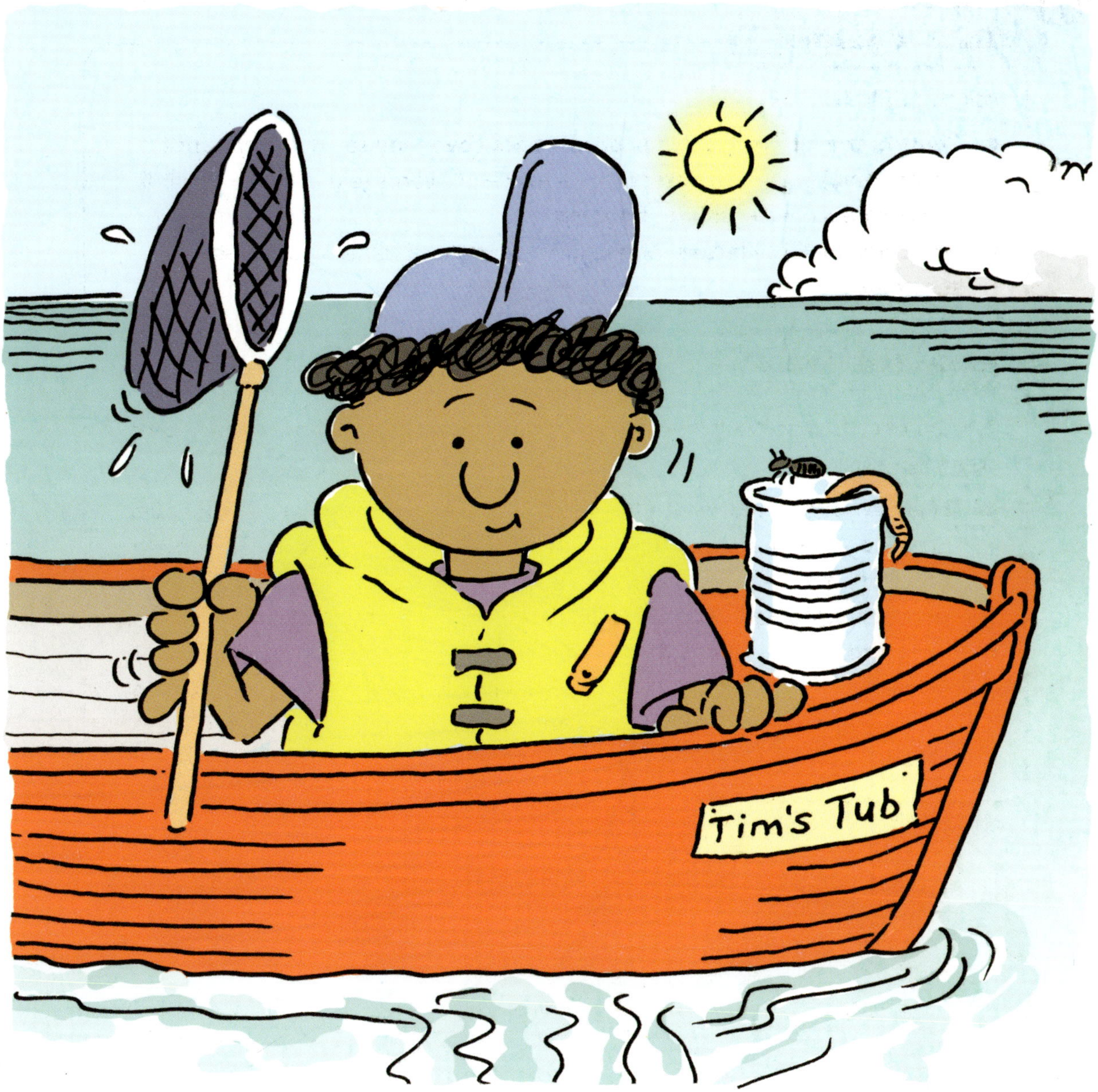

Tim's Dad has a rod and a can.

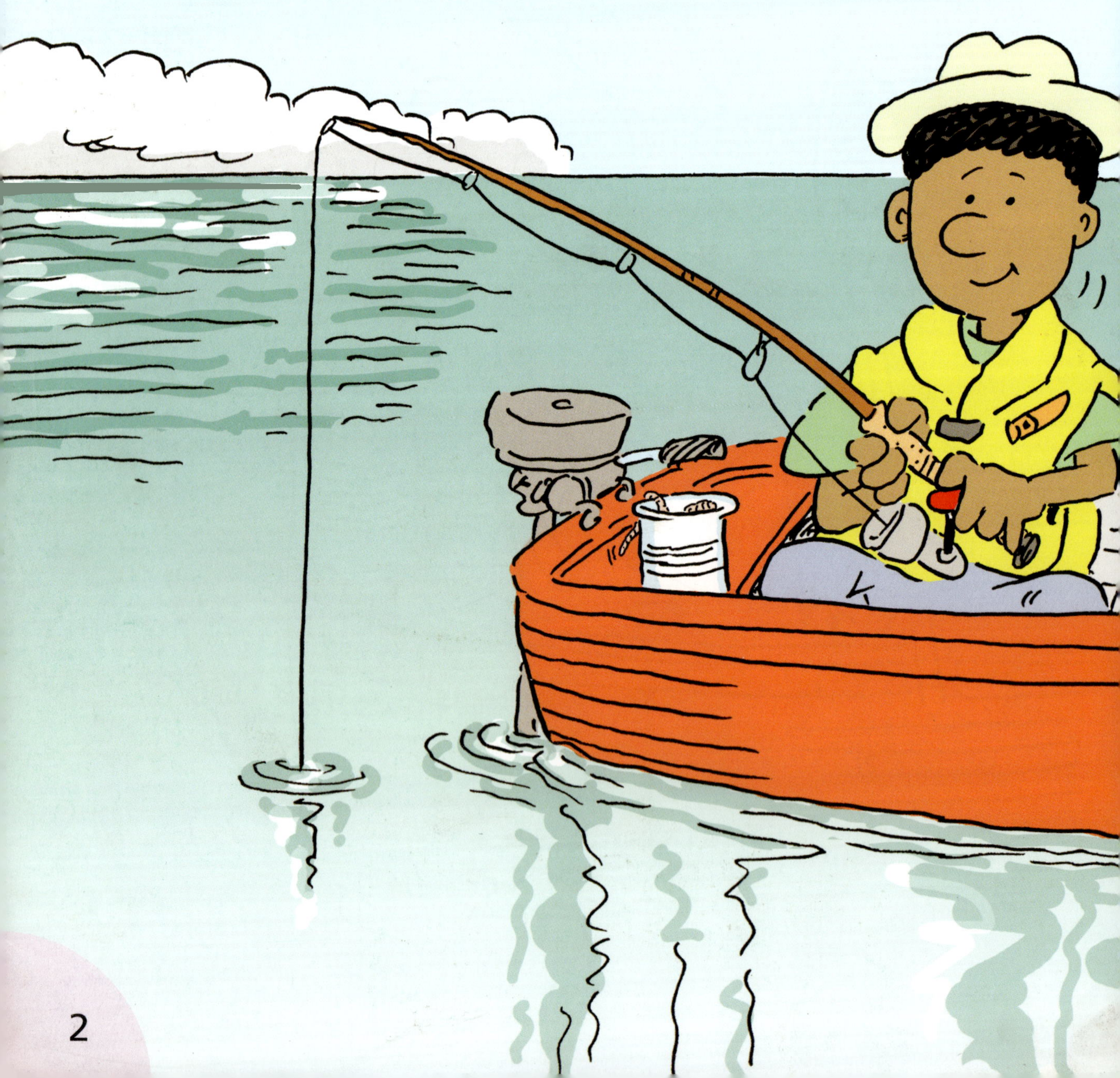

# Tim and Dad sit and sit.

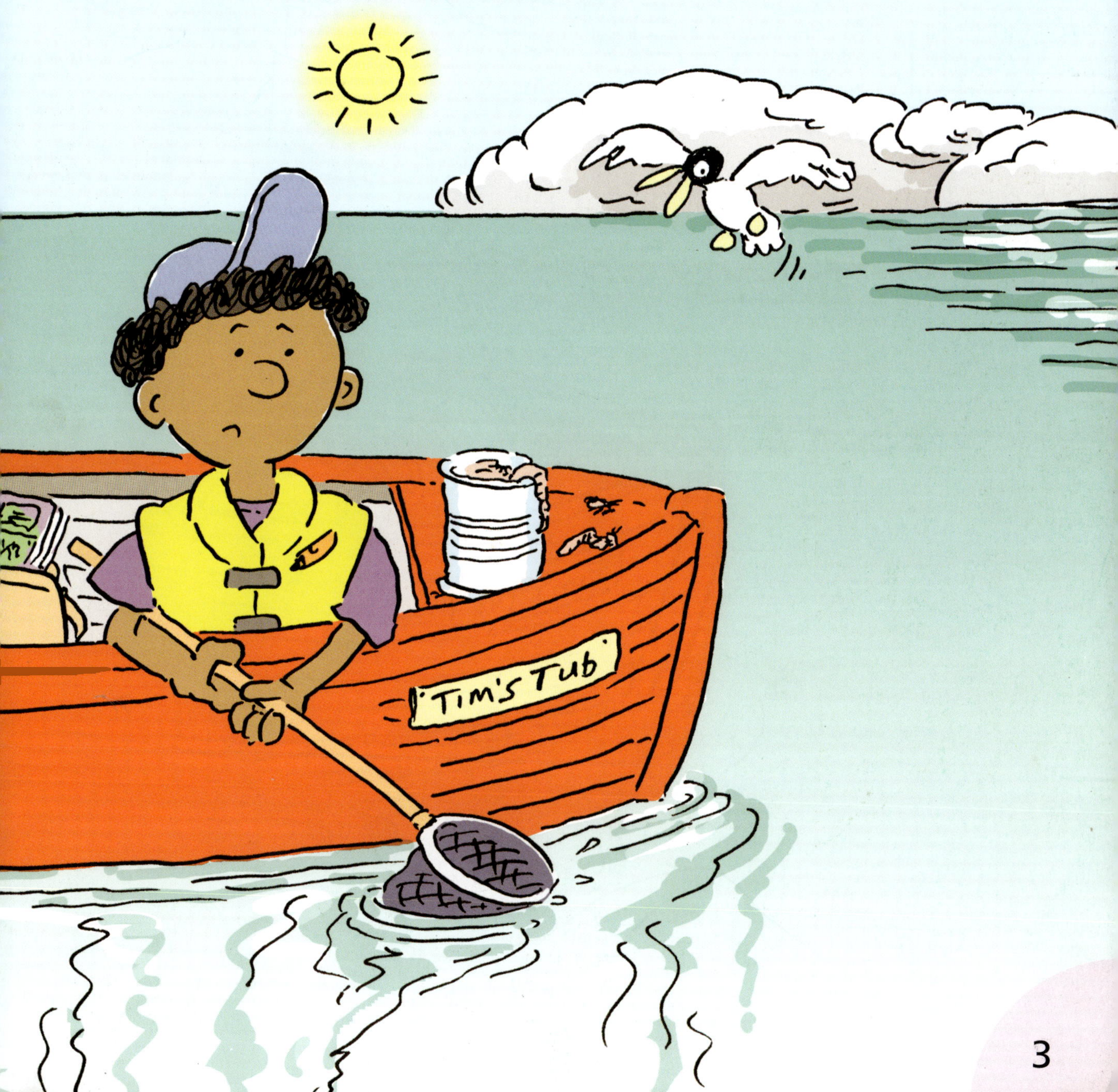

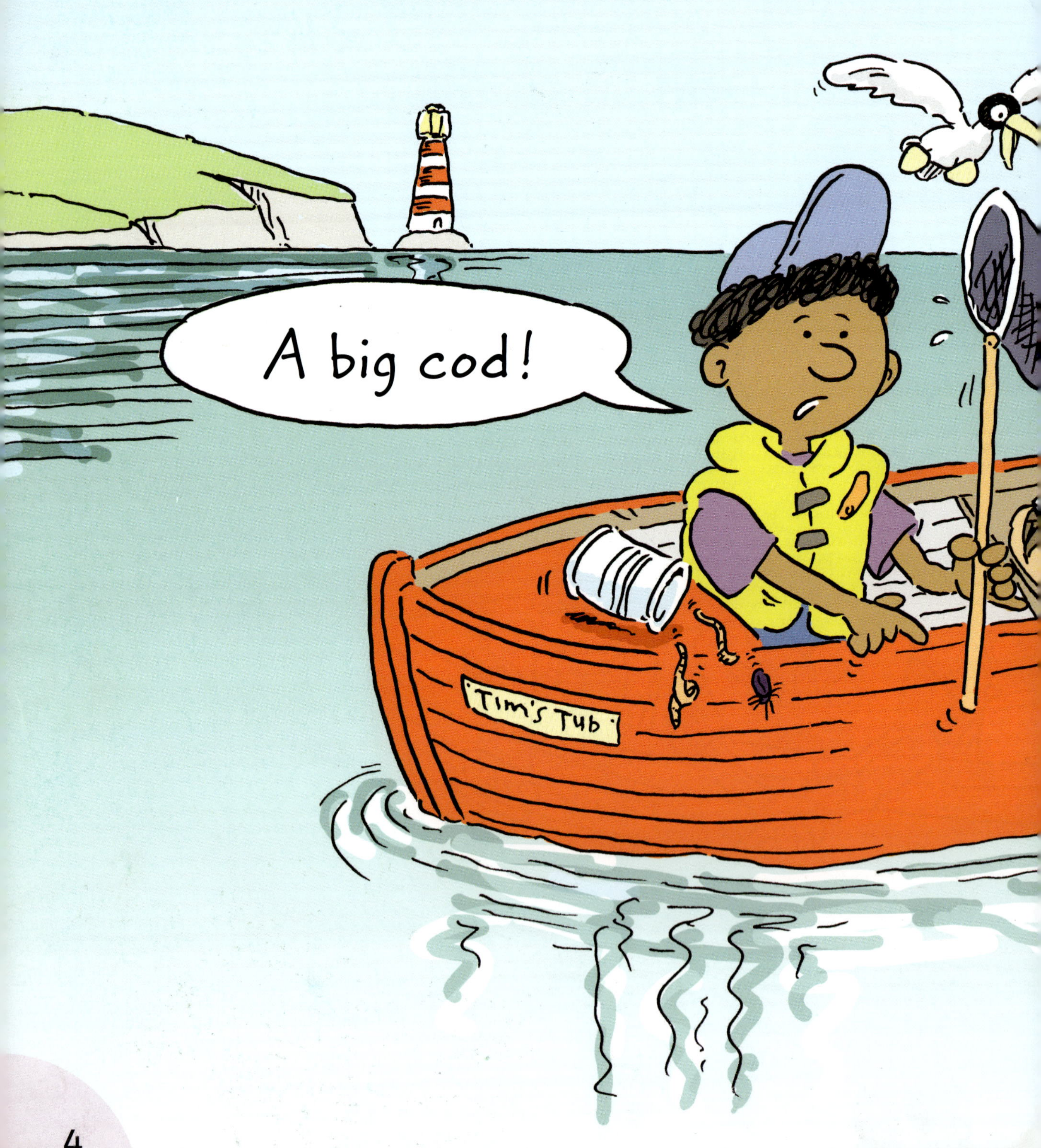

A big cod!
Tim's Tub

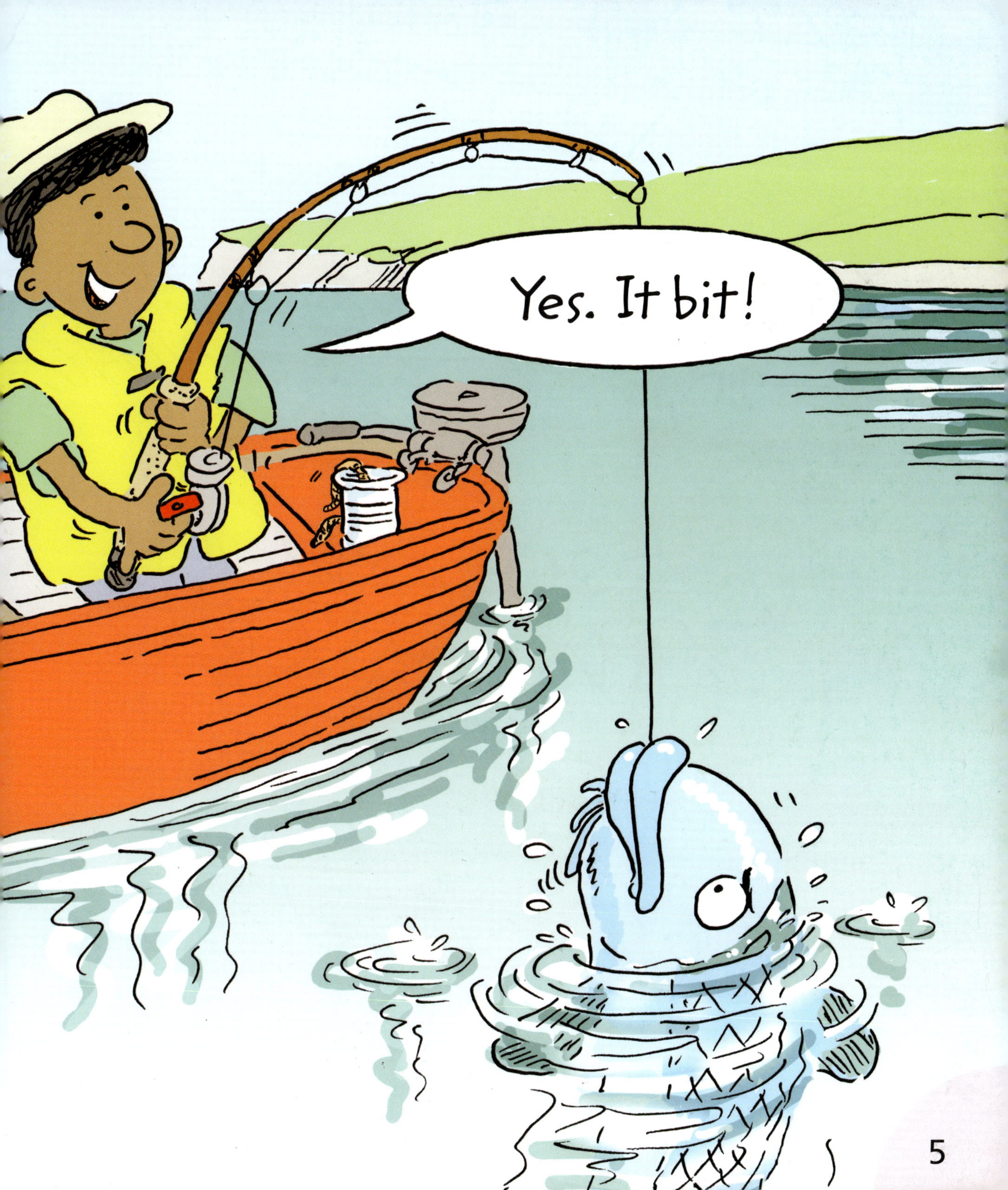
Yes. It bit!

Dad tugs and tugs.

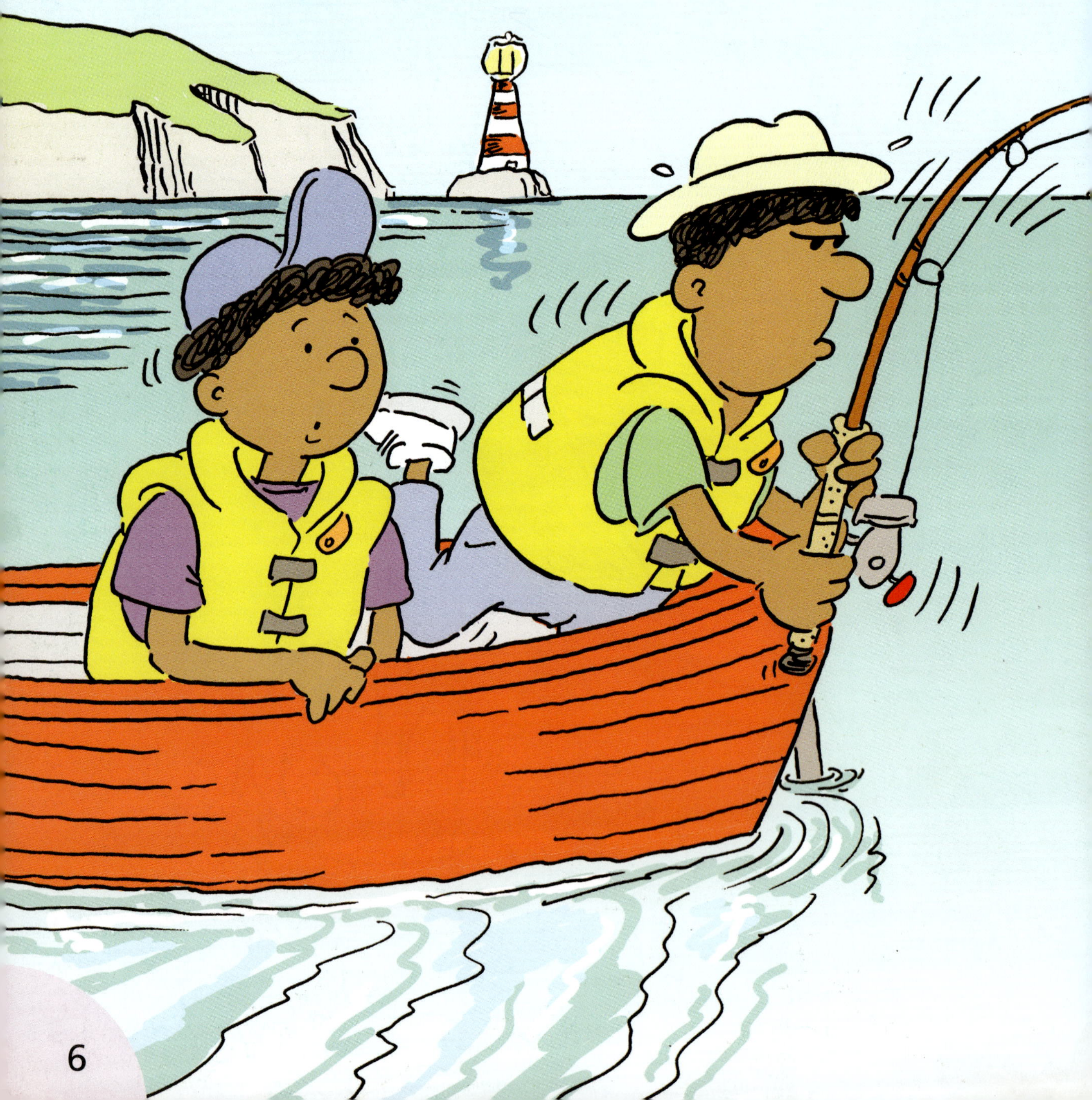

The cod tugs and tugs.

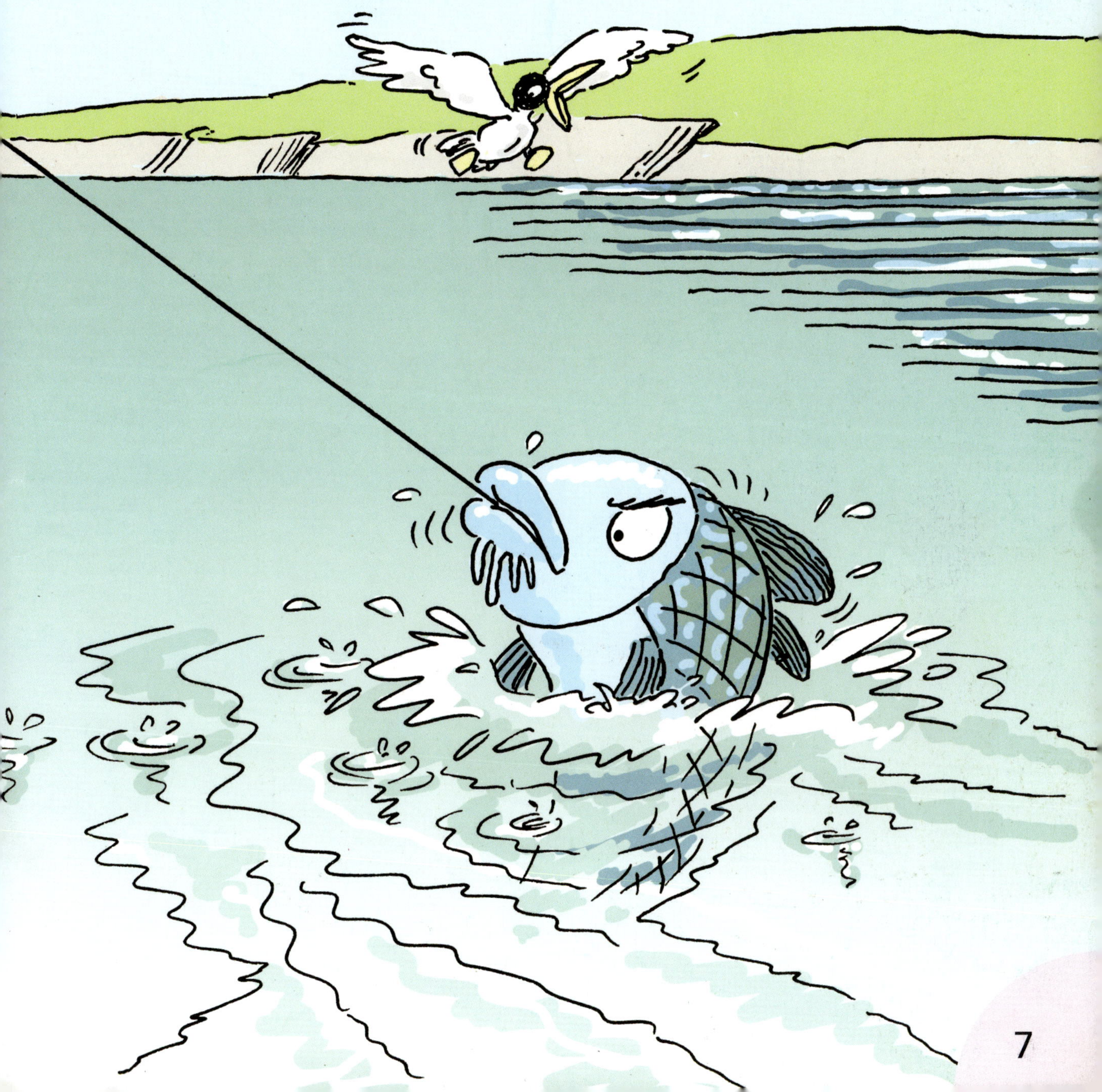

# Dad gets wet.

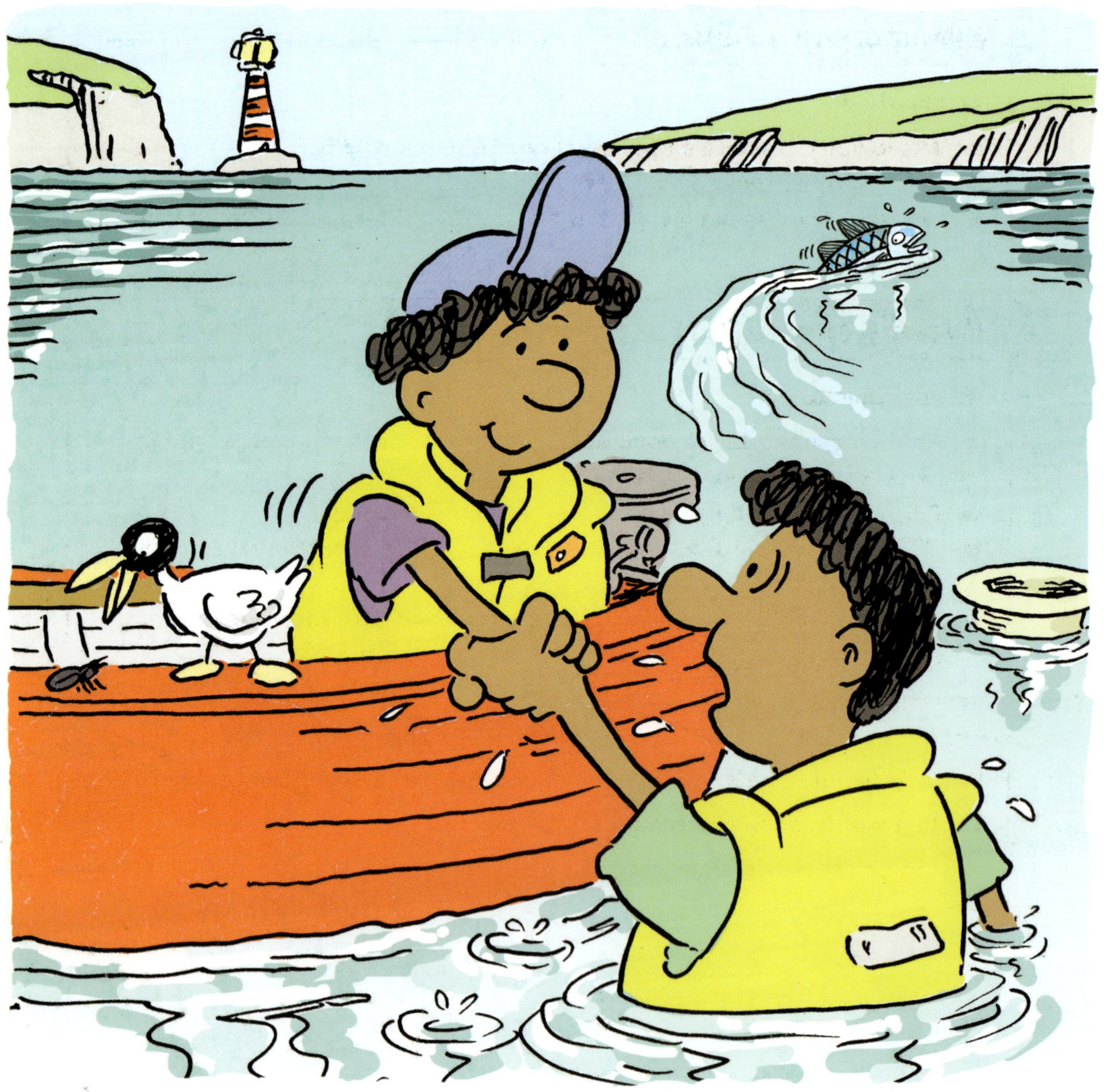